MEMOIRS OF A
Beautiful Disaster

MEMOIRS OF A
Beautiful Disaster

ASHLEY SIMMONS

To order additional copies of this book, contact:
Xlibris
844-714-8691
www.Xlibris.com
Orders@Xlibris.com
827763

Contents

Don Don

Thank you for choosing me When I felt like I was losing me You gave me sight of things I was refusing to seeYou choosing me is helping me to be who I'm supposed to beBecoming your mom was what I was meant to be, you have given me such a purpose that is adding to me like a surplusI look at you and it's my drive to thrive, because of you I have arrived, before it was that I had only survived and felt deprived I see your smile and and it drives me wild I feel so aliveI will always put you first even when I'm at my worst

Star Player

When you met me you were building your line up

I was never your star player though, I never stuck out showing great potential

She became the MVP from the start and even when I showed potential it didn't matter she was already the star player, the rest of us didn't stand chance

We all tried tirelessly tried to show out but it was never good enough

We got called for an assist when she needed a timeout our time was limited when she wanted to get back in and play

We all waited for the day when we could stay in the game, but it was her that kept you tamed

What was so special about this dame, with impeccable game that made the rest of us lame and the same like there was nothing special about our game

Intense

I crave only what's deep and intense

Intense deep conversations where we are both locked in on sharing our views
Deep intense love that goes so much further than love making. That
I feel your heart and feel everything you feel without words just from
our eyes connecting
Deep bonds that makes you feel like you have such a cosmic connection
that if I think of you when we are apart you call or text
Deep loyalty that makes bonnie and clyde look shaky, giving a new
definition to ride or die
I need that intense deep need for when I'm away for a while when I get
back it's like you felt it was way too long be away from another
Deep feeling like we find each other in every lifetime because one can't
survice for what we have
We will always find one another because it can only ever be us
Deep intense passionate sex where it feels like are souls have binded as one
If it's anything else less than that, it's not for me this feels like I'm
robbing my heart
So I ask you ....Can you give me deep/intense

Shit, be so Temporary

He said our chemistry was electric
That my eyes held him captive and he couldn't understand what this was
He kept telling me how he felt like he knew me, all I kept thinking was
could he be my twin flame finally finding me in this life to be his wife,
and save me from the strife, in this tiresome life
I know his face wasn't one I knew before but his presence felt similar
like we danced under the stars in the rain
Could this be what I was waiting for, or just another to pass the time
To my surprise that flame died faster than all the lies you spit, with
your witt

The Curse

Falling for the wrong one is my curse, in life you wish you had a chance to rehearse

Pouring yourself into empty vessels is really the worst the void of expectations is enough to make you want to burst

This crave I have for love will one day leave me in a hurst

My abandonment issues keep wanting to cleave to all I need to leave

When they leave they all take with them a piece of me like a thief

Choosing the same men is becoming a bore and a frustrating chore constantly bringing my trash to the door God knows I just want more

Constantly opening the door for more, to get more less than what I had before, the nice act to lure me in worked for sure, but with time the skeletons come falling out the locked doors

Why I just keep finding thunder while watching others love makes me wonder why I always end up in this blunder looking to feed this hunger

Apology to The Good Men

As a woman we are conditioned to think a man is supposed to be our peace, and fulfill our happiness

We tend to forget that men are too experiencing turmoil that they are told they cannot express because they are men

We forget they have obstacles that they're currently fighting on a daily basis

We forget they may have not healed from past trauma

We forget to be patient that they may have not been taught how to be properly loved

We look to them to be our saviors but sometimes they may need us to be the saving grace

We expect so much of them, but we forget the shared effort on our end

We want to be on his mind to where he wants to always talk to us, but we have forgotten to be thoughtful of his feelings to be considered to be thought of

We forget to listen to their concerns to needs, not just sexually, but what they need for their own sanity

We need to be better with apologizing when we are wrong and take accountability for our words and actions

So on behalf of women that see and understand your a good man and that your needs sometimes are not met I'm sorry

Midnight

He was midnight black, but his aura was brighter than the sun

His smile was whiter than pure untouched snow, but warmer than a summer breeze left you feeling complete ease

He was deeper than than the ocean, he was the universe you didn't know where it started and where it ended but his stars illuminated so bright that your mesmerized and cant stop staring wondering what wonders you could find

He had a way with words that kept you hanging onto every word begging for him to never stop, he calmed my soul in a way never felt before

He touched me with his eyes in a way that left warm with pure euphoria, and sensuality bringing you to ecstasy

His poise was strong and confident, made me feel honored to be in his presence soaking in his beautiful essesnce

It was Never You

Secretly deep down I knew, that it could never be you

Way before I said I was through, I knew this thing between us would never be quite do

I searched for things in you that I knew you could never do, I really was seeking in you what I wanted in another brother, playing like you could be the significant other

You were a substitute for a man I was missing, while it was you I was kissing seeking validation, and confirmation that I was good enough I must say was kind of ruff

I never got closure so I seeked out on a mission, that became a fixation on what I was lacking, to gain my own gratification to bring me to clarification on my miseducation of what I needed to be for my own satisfaction

I became the protagonist in my own story, by my hurting and wanting answers I allowed things that should of never been to be, then looking for why they didn't work

At first I thought it was clever to go about this endeavor but now I see why this could never be

I gained the closure through this crouse game of cat and mouse

On a daily basis our bodies have trillions of different bacterias actively living inside us

We are in a constant state of fight or flight without our knowledge of it

We fight things off without even batting an eyelash

Yet we get a few negative thoughts in our mind and let it crumble us to nothing

Doubting whether we can make it out of this funk, meanwhile the rest of the body is wondering how easy the mind has it

The cells are warriors in a constant war to keep you in good standing

My goal in life is to take my hurt and use for good

Maybe my turmoil to redemption can help some find the light at the tunnel for someone who may have experienced what I have

To let people know that life is hard and that although in life you may not be able to see things changing for better it's up to you to say I can't let this be and I can turn this around

Call of Booty

Laying in this bed watching you play call of duty while waiting for you
to come please this booty

Slow kisses on your neck while stroking your dick, your focus on the
game is making me sick

You got 5 kills on your mission, I'm tryna entice an intermission for my
main mission, Claws in your neck hoping for you to take me off pause

You speak into your mic while I try to speak into yours

You just got a care package with more amo, I working on caring for your
package and emptying your arsenal buss your gun daddy

I'm breaking your concentration while we both work on getting these
head shots

Infidelity

You hold me with your eyes, behind my eyes were true lies, and betrayal
Your hands on my thighs bring me to new highs, this build up was bigger than my lies
My mind running on a way to devise another lie, for the one I grew to despise, while staring into your brown eyes
You grab hold of HIS precious flower and I want nothing more but for you to devour, our time is short, I've only got an hour
Your eyes stay on me as you plunge your manhood into my throat kinda got me feeling like I'm The G.O.A.T or that your the man I need to choose to devote
You slide inside barely fitting, hitting things that have never been touched I scream out Iove this so much
Your pulse on my walls enhancing with each thrust, I want you to slow down it's too much of a rush
Deeper, harder, faster you burst on my ass it looks like plaster
Time to go home and play the devoted wife living the perfect life, all the while filled with strife....

Somtimes in life you need to take a step back and say to yourself, what is it that I'm seeking in myself that keeps attracting things I don't want
You meet people that can't give you what you need mentally or emotionally
The words never match the actions
Things always come up short
It may be that your not truly secure with yourself and you attract others that have the same issues
So you need to take a moment and say let me fix things I'm battling internally so I can attract the partner that I want

Everything that happens to you is a lesson or a blessing
It up to to take that hurt and put it to good work
Or let that hurt bring out your worst

I used to think of ways to put I smile on your face now all I want is to erase the image of your face

It's those moments when you go through things that you really realize that you have no one.

When you dont have anyone to check on you
Send you flowers or visits when your in the hospital
When you can't be out having fun who looks for you
That's when it all sinks in that the people you have around you, aren't
really for you

It was never my birthday if I didnt cut the cake with you it was just a regular day

They haven't been the same since you left

Home only felt like home if you were there now I search for home in others for a lost outcome

You left me long before you left this world, so now my abandonment issues keep me looking for you in others

Losing your love was the greatest lose I've faced in this life

Wrongfully Deflowered

You were a rose a delicate flower never meant to be devoured or wrongfully deflowered left with a nasty scour

It felt like the loneliest hour as you stood over me like a tower, thrashing my sweet flower that day you took all of my power

Dignity, and self worth are now nothing more than a faint memory

Constant strife on how to find a way back only to see this nightmare that doesn't go away when I am awake, feels like its putting my life at stake

I lay here in your bed watching you as lay your head
I gently caress you as I want to address you
as mine, but in this time I can't have you as mine maybe in another life
I could be your wife
In this life I serve another purpose, so I can only have what's on the surface
Wanting a deeper connection and all your affection confined to deep
affliction and contradiction, causing us constant friction
I'm craving your love like an addiction
Our song in my head sounds like a rendition
It could all be so simple, looking as perfect as your dimples, but always
end up more like unwanted wrinkles and pimples

How can someone who has done so little mean so much
Constantly looking for you touch
Can't get your actions to even go dutch, this is becoming too much

Unlimited text just to receive unwanted sexts
Unlimited data for unused communication skills
I thought technology was supposed to make it all better somehow it
seems a lot worst

Mind Games

I wanna know what your love feels like

Although I know I can't have that, and I should really be past that, but in my mind I can't help but reenact that

I need to put you in the past... facts

I wanna feel like your one and only

You compromise my mind from the things you told me

Condoned to living on the side lines, refusing to read in between the lines, listening to all the sweet lines because they sound so divine we go through this all the time it's just playing with my mind

I'm in too deep my feeling have gotten to a place where it's way to steep to make that leap or to think it's possible for a retreat

Left feeling like it's just nothing but a defeat

Filling this void sometimes feels like I'm coming up with a new theory like Sigmoid and Freud

Late nights and pillow talks leaving me wanting more like long walks and future talk

Spending my days with pointless conversations and dates with people I wish were you has me feeling subdued because all I want is you

I cant have you as mine making me feel like it's a crime because this is something that could be so devine but I'm not worth your time

As a woman anything you give me I enhance. You give me your heart
I give you unconditional love
You give me your seed I give you a child
You give me a child I give you a family
You give me a house I make our home
Sooo....why am I chasing you when I'm the real prize

You want me to be thirsty for you attention but you never hydrated me enough to feel thirst in your absence

Dont let men make your body a burial ground when you are meant to be the garden of eden

Just because this chapters ends doesnt mean a more beautiful one isnt about to start
One chapter won't end the story, the same a tree doesn't die because the leaves have fallen

Pretty face thick waist full of grace seems like they all want a taste
They all come with haste bringing nothing but waste begging for an embrace is always the case
Don't waste all that good lace for a nice face only offering things of beer taste

Gone

Her silence spoke volumes her mouth could no longer speak
See for she had finally gotten to her peak
She grew weary and tired
She had spoken one too many times before
Now you have her silence as she makes her way to the door
The pain you gave was too much to endure

Until

Until I find a man that sees my presence as a present I cannot allow myself to give access to their absence of interest and consistency.
Until I find a man with a purpose my only purpose will be me, myself, and I.
Until actions match words I will remain single, cautiously ready to mingle

Seems crazy to still be in love with someone and not want to be with them at the same time.

Upset that they are doing the things the said they were gonna do with you with another while you still hurting and searching for better

It all seems unclear how could this be fair that I'm stuck in despair while your in bliss. You played me and and somehow karma seems to be playing with me

Missing The Signs

Something mesmerizing about the ocean you watch the waves come in and violently hit the shore and knock you down but for some reason it makes you wanna go deeper and be pulled in by that current leaving you helplessly trying to make your way back when you realize you no longer can feel the ocean floor and everyone is in such a distance. Apart of you wants to drift with it and see where it takes you while you know you need to head back to shore

Kind of like love seeing the warning signs but being so caught up you can't let go so you keep it going to where you've got drifted to far and now your drowning, struggling to make your way back to shore with the current hitting you from all directions something that seemed so calming is now a calamity

I've fallen in love with a man that doesnt love me hell he don't even want me

I give him my body when he calls for it at night

I passionately make love to him, and he fucks me without any emotion behind it he's just enjoying the moment

I was never meant to last this long I was pussy that turned to be better than he anticipated so here we are a year in, I'm still just pussy but I see him as so much more than just dick although he is a complete dick

We have no obligations to one another but I feel guilty when someone else tries to talk to me. He on the other hand feels no way about talking to new women

He has every excuse as to why he cant put in any effort to me, although I feel like it's because there is someone else he rather put it in with, he will never tell me the truth thou

 Lilith

Her beauty was breath taking the most beautiful sin ever created
She came as a thief in the night dressed in all white
Giving you the greatest pleasure to the ultimate demise
Her spell made the holiest man turn the biggest sinner where he felt like
he was a winner he fell capture in the human rapture
She gave him the sweetest love feeding him the forbidden fruit
Lilith sent from the pits of hell, a demon sent with an angelic face and
warm embrace turning a holy man into a disgrace
Such a beautiful face with a ugly purpose leaving a man stuck in was it
really worth it risked it all for just one taste never even got the embrace
while falling from grace

Natural Disaster

She's a natural disaster coming unexpectedly sucking you in, spinning you around, then spits you, and after she's gone your still in awe of how powerful she is

It's like men have a sixth sense for when your telling your friends I'm done with him, you instantly get a text about how they wanna be better and fix things
Yet some how those instincts dont kick in to make them do it before you get fed up

Chasing Love in Lust

She was looking for love and caught up in lust

The lust kept drawing her back thinking it was love but when the lust was done the emptiness was all that remained, continuously left unclaimed ·

Searching for love in all the wrong spaces, praying for aces in all the pretty faces, left with jokers that always throw up the deuces and have all the excuses why they can't be the King that gives her the ring

Illuminated with ruminations, and fascinations of the one, causing the despair that feels so unfair

Love seems to be for everyone else but her it was becoming too much to bare the reason was unclear

Beauty in the Mess

There is beauty in your beautiful mess

You have the hurt of love lost

You have optimism of a better stronger love with another

There is strength in all you have overcame

You were meant to break and you managed to crack and not shatter

What you endured added to the woman you were, you never lost a thing, you gained

You evolved from glass to concrete, your solid as a rock its gonna take a lot more for you to be diminshed to nothing

That lesson whatever it may be is your blessing take that with stride and pride, you have gone from a house kitten to a fiery wild lioness queen of the jungle

Your crown wasn't taken it was upgraded for a larger more embellished one

Mind Fuck Me

Fuck my mind and drive me crazy

Intrigue my mind to always want more

Keep me guessing to what may come next like a cliffhanger in a good book

Unlock these levels and win the prize, what a surprise, arousing my mind will make the body follow

I'm a sapiosexual open my mind before trying to open my legs

I'm not just a pretty face, and nice body I'm a Goddess anointed by God

I'm a blessing, and a lesson not your night nurse

Help me unlock my crown chakra and I'll always be yours

Waiting for the one while seeing your exes move on and have everything they promised you is heart breaking
Somehow it hurts more than the hurt they inflicted

My eyes have realized the real lies
You led me to believe it was all real all to see you sealed the deal leading
me to a well that had long gone dry
Leaving me here in despair, it felt so unfair, no pain could ever compare
to that cold glare in your stare

Understand This

When I tell you about my past it's not to bash my past it's for you to understand how I need you to be different than what i had

When i pour my soul out and let you know all of me it's not because I'm bored, it's because I want you to know me better and understand me I want my partner to be my best friend

When I cry, it's not because I'm too sensitive, it's because i don't let many get close to me and you have let me down, and I am disappointed because I expected more of you

When I share my body with you, it's because it's not that I want to get my a release, it's me giving you all my postive energy, me allowing our spirits to bind as one

When I say I love you, it's not just something to say because it seems right in the moment, I truly mean that with every fiber in my body, unconditionally, without boundaries, and limitations

When I say you have my loyalty, i don't say that because it's the right words you need to hear, I truly mean it I will always be by your side, holding you up when you fall, your confidant in times where you need counsel, you are my king and I your queen

I Am The Moon

I want to draw you in and have you distorted as the waves of the ocean
I want to illuminate your life the way I light up the sky leaving you so
fascinated by my soul you can't take your eyes off me
I want to keep you grounded as my pull on gravity to the earth
I want to give you passion you have never felt before keeping you
coming back for more
I want to birth so much life and love into your life that even after death
our souls will always find one another
I am the moon I am wisdom, intuition, birth, death, and reincarnation

Love the stretchmarks on you body, those are tiger stripes for a fierce bitch

Love that lil tummy, and love handles, just makes you better for cuddling, and something extra to grab on to

Love all the parts of you; even though its imperfect your always good enough

The right one with think all your imperfections are perfections

I want to be a constellation
My tale told across the sky
All the here, when's and why
To never be forgotten
To be stared at in awe
After death still luminatating this world with my light

Rainy

There's something about sitting in the rain and having the water hit you
It's like a cleansing washing away all sadness and hurt
Taking away all the negative energy
Your body is crying but its not your tears the ones from the heavens
saying I see your hurt I will cry with you love

Aquarius

The water bearer
I give you nourishment when you thirst
I'm deep enough to draw you in and get lost in
Powerful enough to drown you in my love

I was single before I met you, and happy with my decision to be alone
But being with you I have never felt so lonely
I have never craved affection more from being with you
Being with you, I never felt so unappreciated, and unworthy of love
Being with you I have never questioned my entire being the way I have
from encountering you

So now I'm choosing to never be with you again
Now I will not let you dim my light
Now I will readjust my crown and sit back on my thrown as the
Empress I am
Now I will treat you as the peasant you really are

Teaching myself, self love
So I can later give the best love

I want to be desired
Not just for the nectar of my devine flower
I want you to crave my presence like a drug not just my body at night
Be drawn into my intellect and creative mind like current from the sea
I want my soft heart to warm yours so much your cold in my absence
I want to be your guiding light home when your lost, and your safe
haven when your hurt

Andromeda- The Chained Maiden

Her beauty is her curse
She is a beautiful woman inside and out
But she is more that what meets the eye
Held captive by her exterior
Shakeled and oppressed to an appearance never seen for the true beauty within
These chains wear heavy on her heart
Desired by many, valued by none; while she's searching for the one leading to a lost outcome
Burdened by agony of yearning to be understood
Desperation for her voice to be heard
A slave to all she should be, with hopes of all she strives to be, praying for emancipation longing to be freed is her only decree

Polaris

I should of never asked...
They say don't ask if your not prepared for the answer

I asked about her
She was "The One to get away"
The way he spoke of her so highly and somehow still amazed
I looked in his eyes and saw his pain
That look of regret, when you know what you had, you let it go, nothing compares, and I know I shouldn't dare to compare or even try to fill those shoes.
The way he described how she held his heart, and was the apple of his eyes...
It broke my heart in such a way, that it brought a tear to my eye
It brought me back.
It brought me to think of when I had someone that felt that way about me, and made me feel like I was the only one in the world, to ignite that fire, and awaken his soul
But the way he said what he said made me feel like that fire I ignited in mine wasnt even close to the one she did for him. It was like she opened his third eye, gave him such enlightenment that any other would seem like a dimm lit match in a dark forest, it could never compare
His Polaris the North Star, her love will always bring him home
Without her he is lost
The fire that kept him warm is no more, he is cold and wants to go home
So he waits for the sun to come down so Polaris can bring him home
How can I compare to even try to come near to what she has done for him. I could never be what she is, so what do I do, as my feelings grow for him, but I will always be number 2, i can only occupy his time waiting in line for a spot that will never be mine.
....Polaris

Constellations

The stars all tell a tale
A story not to be forgotten
Plastered across the skies for us to sing their tales in glory
Shining bright in the sky, but slightly dead inside

Gone but never to be forgotten

Confidence

Self-Efficacy-the belief in your ability to accomplish specific tasks

Self confidence- how likely you are to accomplish goals

Self esteem- the belief of your overall worth

Arrogance- the result of insecurity than self confidence, external validation to feel good

So efficacy, confidence, and esteem are the goals ✓✓✓ and arrogance is ✗✗✗

Now when you have no way of figuring out how to get to the good things with no real guide on the thin line of good and bad

Now I believe I can accomplish anything I put my mind to positive thoughts = positive results; I believe in myself so therefore ability to do is in my favor; ok I believe in my self so therefore my worth golden so I then conduct myself to walk around with confidence. But somehow that seems like it would come off as arrogance or maybe I'm missing something

This is seeming real thin line between love and hate

Threesomes are Fun

I'm having a threesome with insomnia and ruminations
I'm in real deep
My ruminations keep my mind going constant questions, & overwhelming
thoughts that have been fought all day leaving me in pure dismay
The insomnia keeps me looking at the clock tick, tick, tick, tock how
do I make it stop
My mind with ruminations constantly going, running to go nowhere
like a gerbil on a wheel where the fuck am I really going, what the fuck
am I doing, full speed yet not moving and God damn inch
How do I break up with the most consistent relationship I've had in yrs
I know I can always count on them to keep me company at night, as
we fight to not somehow not meet daylight

What Will it Be

I can be sweet as sugar, or sour like salt
I can be as warm as summer, or the coldest winter ever
I can be as loyal as dog, or a relentless raging bitch
The choice is your, you get what you give

Nothing Regular About Your Black Sis

She said she was just regular black

I looked back like no sis there's nothing regular about your black
Your black is beautiful
Your black is bold
Your black is strength and determination
Your black always gets knocked down but always bounces right back
Your black is rich in melanin and sweet like berries
Your black get overlooked but makes you work harder to prevail
They pay money for that regular black, dying to look your regular appearance

Be Fair

You say my black is beautiful, yet you pick the latinas, chinos, and white over my sunkissed shades of brown

You want us to be strong and independent, yet those are the same things you leave us for

You want me to be educated and have views on topics, yet when I share my views I'm too opinionated

We want when I'm hurting that we can shed a tear, and vent

We want to be be able to express our feelings when frustrated or feeling passionate about something and not be called angry or aggressive, make excuses for us the way you do them

We want to be catered to and treated like a delicate flower the way you do them

We want to be the trophy wife, here to be cute and fun

We want to submit but you give nothing to submit to

I Submit

You are my King, the head, you have the eyes of the vision of what we can become, your mind is strong, and I follow your lead for where the head goes, I the body shall follow

I am your Queen, I am your neck and spine
As your neck I set you in the right direction incase you get off track
As your spine I am the support, I hold you up, never letting you fall short of your greatness

I am the ying to your yang our souls entwined, one sound, one heart beat

I submit to you my King
I stand behind and beside you; to never walk through this life alone
I want to bless your royalty with my loyalty

Do You Really See Me

Are you attracted to me, not my face and body, Me on the inside
Are you attracted to my heart that pours out love and devotion
My mind full of intellect and questions
My potential, the woman I am trying to be
My strength to overcome as much as I did and not fold or give up
Do I inspire more than just an erection, inspiring you to be a better man
because you want to be man you think I deserve

Cut, Erase, Delete

I still feel dirty many days
Scrubbing my skin til it feels raw while I bathe
I still feel the fear I had that day
I can still taste the tears on my lips
I look in the mirror and still see the blood on my shirt
It's been 16yrs but still feels fresh
I feel shame, and place blame why it all happened
My subconscious still makes me feel like the world can see all my ugly parts I try to bury
I still feel like damaged goods, and unworthy of love
They say time heals wounds but mine are still raw
I've tried my hardest to suppress these memories hoping it could disappear but it won't
It's like a bad movie without the option of edit
I want to fix it ctrl +z, ctrl + z nope still won't come undone.

Potential Get You Every Time

When I look at you a see more than just a man
I look in your eyes I see your passion, and love burning inside
I see your greatness, all that you haven't yet become
I see you as a loving father to your future children
I see you being a good husband, and a provider
I see your mind its strong, and clever, always learning
I see all you can be and possibly will become.
But I feel like all I see is not for me. It's for someone else. Someone who wows you, who you can't get off your mind
I'm what you lust, what you crave at night, thravising inside my yoni in the wee hours of the night, when you really want another. I'm a substitute til the one to unlock your chakras arrives

Survivor

The definition of this word:
1. A person who survives, especially a person remaining after an event in which others died.
2. A person who copes well with difficulties in life.

Survivor
I hate being defined as a survivor.
The word just doesn't seem to fit.
Something else should be what defines a person whom had gone through traumatic events.
Survivor
The word sounds triumphant
But what I survived I can't show praise to
Survivor
When I think of the word it gives the same affect as the word Champion, but what have I won. I get flashbacks of what I survived and I feel shame and dismay.
Survivor
Some how it seems more like entrapment
Stuck in your nightmares that don't go away
Survivor
I survived sexual assualt and domestic abuse
I don't want to celebrate this, I don't feel triumphant. I want to forget, I want want to suppress it so deep down it's like it never happened
I want it all to go away
The shame, the fear, the hurt, the memory to go away
Can I survive that?
Can my survival make it go away
Can my survival erase the memory and make me whole again

Reincarnation

I died
I broke into a million pieces scattered across the universe

I felt as small as an atom in space, its was dark with specks of light in the far distance, no oxygen I couldn't even breath

It was the beginning of my rebirth but unlike Christ it took a bit more than 7 days for my resurrection, it took a bit more to bring the pieces back together, and return to earth

I came back as cracked glass, I was together but you could see all the flaws
The cracks are slowly mending back together making me whole.

Now I love my cracks now, before I died I tried to hide those imperfections, now I take pride in my strides and wear them proudly remembering how I overcame, I fought and won, and I'm here still, still pushing, still fighting, still hoping and dreaming. I'm a Warrior, an Amazon, I was never at anyone's whims, I came, and I conquered, and now I look forward to my next conquest

No one

She is not the girl that gets the happy ending
She is not the girl that get to be the happy wife
She is not the girl that has it all
She is not the girl who has friends
She is not the girl who gets to be loved
She is not the girl you fight for because you cant bare to lose her
She is not the girl that things come easy to

She is the girl you have fun with, before you settle down
She's the good girl that no one wants
She is the girl who gives unconditional love, to never be loved in return
She is the girl who is always loyal, to always be cheated on
She's the girl that no one gives a chance to understand or get to know her
She's the girl that smiles while she is dying inside
She's the girl that everyone comes to; to fix it all but when she cries never a shoulder to lean on or a ear to listen

She is lonely
She is broken
She is always forgotten and left out
She is....no one

Self Love in this Generation is a Joke

Learning self love in a generation of selfishness and loss of chivalry has to be the hardest thing ever

You talk yourself up with the affirmations

You are smart

You are loyal

You are strong

You deserve to be loved

You can do anything you put your mind to

To go out into the world and meet men that make you feel like you aren't worth a call, text, or any effort of courting whatsoever.

You pursue them instead of them pursue you. I should take them on dates, and buy them things, make them feel like a king, all for them to be getting all this from other woman.

It's a competition may the best woman win, or continue competing until you grow tired of pouring yourself in a boy in a mans body, with insecurities that far surpass the ones that keep you up at night.

Growing up your taught to keep a man, you cook, clean, wash, iron, always keep yourself together, be loyal; today you do all that have a good job, multiple degrees, be supportive and still not be worth the effort.

Letter to My Dad

To my father the greatest man I know. I know I'm not perfect and sometimes hard to love. But I'm a overly greatly everyday for the father that I was blessed with. You have always pushed me to be my best self, you have loved me unconditionally, you made me strong. You always made sure I was no ones damsels in distress, I get the damn thing done. I have pride in who I am, and know I am more than my skin color. You told me I came in this world with two strikes against me one being black and two being a woman so I will always have to be just that much better just to be an equal. I value all you have taught, I love you so much that it hurts, and I thank you everyday for a the lessons you have taught. You are my everything, what I say can't hold up to the man you are. I couldn't of asked for a better father I am truly blessed beyond words

I Wish Upon A Star

I was told if you want something bad enough speak it into existence and you will receive it so here is me throwing it into the universe

I wish upon a star for the perfect man

He will be kind and loving
He will have a smile to light up my life
His laugh will be infectious
He will put our love above all
He will be driven and push me to be my best self as I will do the same for him
He will be a good husband, father, son making sure his family is always cared for and feels his love and support
He will accept me flaws and all and love me unconditionally
He will communicate with me in healthy ways
He will not turn his back on me or our family
Together we will raise a family to respect and uplift each other, no one will ever feel alone because our support will help build them up for greatness
I wish that next man is the last man I ever will be with
I wish we can grow old together
I wish for us to watch our family grow over time, mentally, spiritually, emotionally
I wish any generational curses will be broken with us

The Makings of A Woman

Her body is a book the spine holds the weight of the world; holding her upright and together, each page tells a story of hopes, dreams, fears, and past failures

Her eyes are as deep as the ocean, that current drawing you in so swiftly you don't know how you came back from it

Her spirit is like the wind as calming as a summer breeze yet as wild as a hurricane

Her heart has been shattered like glass, and yet somehow still pours out love endlessly

Her lips full and soft uttering sweet nothings into your ears, she has a way with words that can awaken a dragon, and also lay him down to rest.

Her mind is like the moon, luminous enough to light up your life, powerful enough to move the oceans, sensual enough to keep you coming back for more

Page Turner

Let me open my book for you to explore me word by word line by line
You run your fingers up my spine ever so gently, and firmly go deep inside
You hang on to every word waiting to see what comes next; you don't
want put me down you want to reach that climax
It's building you up, you want to go deeper
The suspense is too much, your almost there, but you don't want to
reach the end not just yet, as you lick your finger turning the next page
Here we are it's almost the end, yet you still want more so here we go,
time to dive back in, that was just the prequel of our sequel

May I...

I want to stimulate your mind to where you crave our conversations

I want to awaken parts of you, you didn't know existed

Let me take your pain and replace with pleasure, right all the wrongs enhance you to make you better

I want our souls to bind as one to where no words need to be spoken but it is all understood

I wanna know you so well I can look deep into your eyes to feel what you feel

I want our bond to be so strong nothing can lead either to stray from one another

Her

She is more than just a pretty face
She is more than a nice smile
She is more than just a vessel for your release
She is more than just a good time, not a toy to picked up and played
then left on the shelf

Her smile hides many secrets, and masks the hurt inside
Her eyes hold back many tears, they tell a deep story of triumph from strife
Her mind is ever growing, always thinking of what's next, and new to
conquer
Her body is the garden of eden, it gives life, love, pleasure, and strength
continuously evolving to adapt to the ever changing world
Her heart is pure filled with love, that pours onto all she clings to, it is
also filled with sadness of betrayal, disappointment, and abandonment

So when you call her pretty, and sexy you insult her. She is more than
just her physical she is a force to be wreckened with

5 Yrs....

Today makes 5 years since you have left us.

5 yrs not hearing your voice

5 yrs not seeing your face or holding your hand

5 yrs without your tight hugs as you say I LOVE YOU 100x,

5 yrs missing your songs and stories

5 yrs not smelling your cologne

5 yrs your garden has gone untouched,

5 yrs for the weeds to thrive.

5 yrs for us to fall apart,

5 yrs your not here to keep us together.

5 yrs yet it feels like yesterday, the time has not healed this wound.

5 yrs of no holidays, and birthdays with you.

5 yrs i wish i would go back, have a few more talks with you.

5 yrs although sometimes it felt like i lost you before that. The abandonment started yrs before.

5 yrs not watching baseball

5 yrs i can't call out Grandpa

5 yrs i lost greatest love i ever had

5 yrs of missing you

The Atom

Atom: noun
1. The basic unit of a chemical element
2. Atoms as a source of energy
3. An extremely small amount of a thing or quality

Life is like an atom filled with nothing but + &- that determine whether your stable to be alone or you need to either add or take away something which can change all properties or stay the same. Your the neutron surrounded by + &- charges. Sometimes you need to make a bond to make you stable, and sometimes you can be stable enough to be okay alone because that valent shell is just so full.

Ionic Bond: noun
1. When a positively charged ion forms a bond with a negatively charged ion and one atom transfers electron
2. Two opposite charges attract each other and one atom gives up one or more electrons while the other atom gains electrons

Ionic bonds are sometimes just like people you make relationships toxic people sometimes people attach and transfer their - electrons and while they may gain from attaching to your valent shell while bonded you lose some of those + charges making you feel more - than anything.

Covalent Bond: noun
1. A chemical bond that involves the sharing of electron pairs between atoms; the stable balance of attractive and repulsive force between atoms.

Covalent bonds are sharing + & - charges. That mutualized sharing of a bond where you aren't really losing any + or gaining -. It's attaching yet coexisting to live a bit more harmonious. Nothing really being gained or lost from bond. It's the strong healthy kind of bonds you want to make in life.

You pray that all the - charges are more like Hydrogen bonds. Weak and easily broken. You don't want all that - to take away from all the + you have in your valent shell making you become more -. Stopping you from that full potential.

Polar Covalent Bonds: noun
1. Bond between two atoms where the electrons forming the bonds are equally distributed, causing one side slightly more positive and the other side slightly more negative.

Polar Covalent Bonds seem like a healthy relationship the equal effort being put in to make things keep a balance. Sometimes you may feel a little - and you need that + charge to help you feel a bit more stable and vice versa.

Non Polar Covalent Bonds: noun
1. Bonds that equally share the bond of electrons; are when electronegatives of the two atoms are equal.

You never want to attach your - charges to more -charges, although usually two negatives are supposed to give you a positive. In life most cases the adding of the -charges to more - charges can be a recipe for disaster.

I'm an atom hoping to be an element who's valent shell wants to be full. To be ok alone and maybe one day polar covalent bond. Having balance if attached to another.
But for now just trying to get that valent shell full

Deck of Cards

It's crazy how life is really like playing cards. You shuffle looking for your ♠ or ♥ and somehow end up with ♦.

You keep trying to come up with 21 all end up coming up short. Praying for that Royal Flush finding yourself getting craps.

Too many ♦ acting like ♠ and really trying to breakdown the ♛ trying to lessen her value and knock over the crown. So she can settle for less than she deserves. Accepting the bare minimum because they dont want to put in the effort.

Sometimes you get close with a Jack or Ace which treat you the way you want yet can't fully give you it all. One foot in and one out.
You shuffle over and over with high hope's that your gonna get 21. Its your time to shine this is the moment you been waiting for. To flip that card and get a 2 or 3.

Some times its UNO your down to the last card and boom draw 4, skip, reverse and your back in the game. Chasing people that dont want to be caught. Hit with unnecessary bullshit or other people's baggage suffering consequences of things you had nothing to do with.

The Tears Behind The Smile

Inside she cries wishing the smile she wears on the outside can ease the pain she feels inside.

Constant disparity taking over within. The excessive smiles and laughs to hide the pain within.

Hoping no one can see all the pain that haunts her.

Trying to be perfect so no one can see how broken and disheveled she is.

Loneliness is eating her up inside. Wanting someone to be there but fear of letting people in. Hurt by many playing the part to care but using it all to further break her down.

Made in the USA
Middletown, DE
10 April 2021